DESIGNING
CITY TRANSPORT

BY KATE CONLEY

CONTENT CONSULTANT
Nigel Wilson, PhD
Massachusetts Institute of Technology
Professor Emeritus

Core Library

An Imprint of Abdo Publishing
abdopublishing.com

Cover image: Double-decker buses in London, England,
can accommodate many passengers.

abdopublishing.com

Printed in the United States of America, North Mankato, Minnesota
022018
092018

THIS BOOK CONTAINS
RECYCLED MATERIALS

Cover Photo: Marco Govel/Shutterstock Images
Interior Photos: Marco Govel/Shutterstock Images, 1; Adam Geller/AP Images, 4–5; Everett
Historical/Shutterstock Images, 6; Mahathir Mohd Yasin/Shutterstock Images, 8; Shutterstock
Images, 11, 27, 32–33, 35, 45; Mark Herreid/Shutterstock Images, 14–15; Roschetzky Photography/
Shutterstock Images, 17; Red Line Editorial, 19, 30; David Zalubowski/AP Images, 21; Clari
Massimiliano/Shutterstock Images, 24–25, 43; Christina Felsing/iStockphoto, 38

Editor: Maddie Spalding
Imprint Designer: Maggie Villaume
Series Design Direction: Claire Vanden Branden

Library of Congress Control Number: 2017962642

Publisher's Cataloging-in-Publication Data

Names: Conley, Kate, author.
Title: Designing city transport / by Kate Conley.
Description: Minneapolis, Minnesota : Abdo Publishing, 2019. | Series: Inside modern cities |
    Includes online resources and index.
Identifiers: ISBN 9781532114809 (lib.bdg.) | ISBN 9781532154638 (ebook)
Subjects: LCSH: Engineering design--Juvenile literature. | Transportation engineering--
    Juvenile literature. | Transportation--History--Juvenile literature. | City planning--
    Juvenile literature. | Cities and towns--Juvenile literature.
Classification: DDC 624.023--dc23

CONTENTS

ON THE MOVE

On weekday mornings, traffic zips along freeways in Minneapolis, Minnesota. But not all the commuters are in cars, buses, or trains. Some have a different way to get to work. They strap on helmets, hop on their bicycles, and head to the Midtown Greenway.

The Greenway is a paved path tucked snugly in an old railroad trench. It runs for 5.5 miles (8.9 km). For years, the railway had been rarely used. After much planning, Minneapolis residents and leaders turned the trench into a bicycle freeway.

Today, more than 5,000 cyclists use the Greenway each day. It connects neighborhoods

The Midtown Greenway is an easy way for cyclists to get around Minneapolis.

with downtown Minneapolis. The trail runs below street level. This means cyclists can pass under city streets without stopping. Bicycle-only bridges and on/off ramps ensure riders have a safe trip.

CHANGING VIEWS

Projects such as the Greenway have become popular. They reflect new ideas about transportation systems. In the past, most systems centered on cars. Huge networks of roads and highways sprang up in the 1950s. They made it possible for many people to commute quickly through an area.

Under the car-focused transportation system, traveling long distances became easier. Cities began to sprawl outward. Instead of using many side streets, cars were funneled onto a few high-speed roads. Mass transit, which includes public transportation options such as subways and buses, was a low priority. Walking or bicycling was often difficult and dangerous.

Highways are still important transportation systems. But today, many cities are also investing in other forms of transportation. New transportation systems will allow people to get to work, shops, or restaurants by walking or bicycling rather than driving. Updating a city's transportation system does not happen quickly. It takes years of planning, engineering, and building.

PLANNING THE SYSTEM

City and state governments create most transportation systems. Employees who do this work are called transportation planners. They design many types of systems, from highways to bicycle routes.

In modern cities, many transportation options are often available to commuters.

Transportation planners begin a project by studying data. If car traffic is too heavy, planners may add lanes for car pools or buses. If train cars are too crowded, expanded routes and extra stops may help. If crossing the street on foot is dangerous, planners may widen curbs or add pedestrian islands in the middle of the street.

Planners must also think about how the transportation system will affect nearby homes and businesses. For example, building a new highway might make it easier for people to get to offices and shops. But the noise from speeding cars may bother people who live nearby.

BRINGING IN THE ENGINEERS

Transportation planners work closely with civil engineers. The engineers turn a planner's ideas into a workable design.

MEASURING TRAFFIC LEVELS

Traffic levels are measured in many ways. Sometimes levels are measured manually. A person stands outside and tallies pedestrians, bicycles, or cars that go past. Another tool is a tube filled with compressed air that sits on the surface of a roadway. Each time a car drives over the tube, a machine tallies the car and its speed. Infrared sensors, thermal devices, or radio signals can also be used to record pedestrian and cyclist traffic.

Their first job is to study the site. They look at its soil, drainage, and elevations. This helps the engineers decide which materials and building methods will work best.

Next, engineers apply science to the transportation planner's design. For example, a transportation system may require a bridge. Engineers consider how much weight the bridge should be able to support. This weight can vary greatly,

When developing transportation systems, such as Japan's high-speed trains, engineers make sure infrastructure is strong.

depending on whether it is a pedestrian bridge or a highway bridge.

Engineers create their designs as a set of detailed drawings on a computer. Each drawing has a different perspective. A plan view shows the site from directly above. Elevations show the site from the front, rear, or side. A cross section is an elevation with the exterior removed. This allows builders to see a site's levels.

BUILDING BEGINS

The building crew uses the engineer's drawings as a set of directions. The directions give the crew details of the project. The crew uses the drawings to learn how wide to make a lane or where the traffic signals should be placed.

Crews also use the drawings for earthwork. Earthwork is a part of the construction process. Existing roads or rails are removed. Heavy machines level and compact the soil to form a stable base. Crews then install utilities, such as electric lines and sewers. Then the final surface can be installed.

Transportation systems often take several months or even years to build. They can cost millions of dollars. But they are an essential part of any city. Roads and rails bring commuters to work, food to grocery stores, and children to school. They are the lifeblood of the world's cities.

STRAIGHT TO THE
SOURCE

Jane Jacobs was a Canadian writer and urbanologist. She studied cities, focusing on their problems and ways to plan for the future. Jacobs criticized the changes taking place in cities in the 1950s, which made cars the priority instead of pedestrians. She shared her views in a 1958 article:

> *The user of downtown is mostly on foot, and to enjoy himself he needs to see plenty of contrast on the streets. He needs assurance that the street is neither interminable nor boring, so he does not get weary just looking down it. . . . Narrow streets, if they are not too narrow (like many of Boston's) and are not choked with cars, can also cheer a walker by giving him a continual choice of this side of the street or that, and twice as much to see. The differences are something anyone can try out for himself by walking a selection of downtown streets.*

> Source: Jane Jacobs. "Downtown Is for People." *Fortune.* Time, 1958. Web. Accessed September 21, 2017.

Point of View

How does Jacobs view the place of streets within cities? What does she think people who live and work in cities value most about their environment?

DRIVING THERE

Today, 11 million Americans commute an hour or more to work each day. They use apps to determine their routes based on traffic conditions. And the Global Positioning System (GPS) makes finding new places easier than ever. But it has not always been that way. In 1900, few Americans owned cars. Cars were too expensive for average families.

That all changed in 1913. In that year, Henry Ford introduced a new method of building cars called the assembly line. It made cars cheaper and easier to build. More people could afford them. But driving was a challenge. Gas stations were hard to find. People had to

Many people around the world prefer driving over other forms of transportation.

buy gas out of barrels at grocery or hardware stores. And hardly any paved roads existed between towns.

As car ownership grew, so did demand for better roads. Driving gradually became practical, easy, and more affordable. By 1930, more than half of all American families owned a car. They had the freedom to travel long distances whenever they wanted to.

WILLIAM P. ENO

In the early 1900s, roads were chaotic. Horses, pedestrians, bicyclists, streetcars, and automobiles all shared the road. Speed limits, street signs, and driver's licenses did not exist. Accidents were common. Businessman William P. Eno wanted to change that. In 1900, he suggested placing a stop sign at every intersection. It was a revolutionary idea. Eno went on to create many other innovations that made driving safer. For his work, Eno is often called the Father of Traffic Safety.

HIGHWAY SYSTEMS

While roads improved, the modern US highway system was not built until after

Modern highway systems make cities and towns easily accessible.

World War II (1939–1945). In 1956, Congress passed the Federal-Aid Highway Act. Its design called for 41,000 miles (66,000 km) of highways. The highway system would connect every US city with 100,000 people or more. Today, this gives Americans a fast and easy way to travel the entire country.

The US network of highways is heavily used. More than 260 million vehicles traveled on US roads in 2015.

THE TROUBLE WITH HOV LANES

While many people cite the benefits of HOV lanes, not everyone is a fan. Some drivers believe their tax dollars helped pay for the HOV lanes, so they should be able to use them, too. To address this complaint, many cities are making changes. Some programs allow drivers without passengers to use HOV lanes for a fee. And during off-peak hours, the HOV lanes are often open to all cars.

Many cities now offer high-occupancy vehicle (HOV) lanes. These cities encourage carpooling by allowing cars with one or more passengers to use these special lanes. This allows people to avoid traffic and get to their destinations faster.

In order to determine whether it would be worthwhile to add new HOV lanes to existing roads, engineers predict how many commuters might use them. They do this by studying driving patterns. If they find that many drivers carpool, they may decide to add an HOV lane.

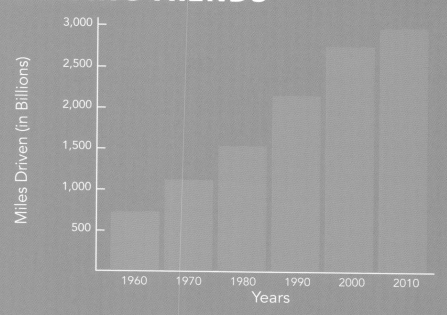

DRIVING TRENDS

Since 1960, the US Department of Transportation has been keeping detailed records about the number of miles driven on US highways. What trend do you notice in the above graph? What are some possible reasons for the trend?

Another change that has affected city transport is the creation of ride-hailing services. In this system, private drivers give rides in their own cars to paying customers. Smartphone apps connect drivers and riders. The best-known ride-hailing services are Uber and Lyft. Seven percent of all young adults between the ages of 18 and 29 use ride-hailing services daily or weekly.

TRAFFIC ENGINEERS

Roads need to be safe and easy to use. That job falls to traffic engineers. They oversee the nation's massive network of roads. They work on a variety of tasks. They may look at an intersection with many accidents. They may decide that something simple, such as a stop sign, would be enough to reduce accidents. Or they may need to redesign the entire intersection to keep it safe.

Traffic engineers also use technology, such as smart traffic lights. Smart traffic lights can reduce wait times at stoplights and keep traffic moving. These lights sense how much traffic passes through an intersection. Their timing can then be adjusted based on real-time traffic conditions.

Smart traffic lights vary the amount of time it takes to pass through an intersection. For example, a stoplight may take 120 seconds to cycle through its red, yellow, and green lights. But if traffic picks up, the green light stays on longer. The cycle time might increase to

Dynamic message signs can alert drivers to road conditions and upcoming construction.

150 seconds. This keeps traffic moving smoothly and reduces travel times.

Dynamic message signs are another technology traffic engineers rely on. These electronic signs hang above highways. They give drivers stuck in traffic an estimate of how long it will take to reach different exits. This estimate can change by the minute, depending on the traffic. Workers watch dozens of cameras positioned above the roads to make their time estimates each day.

SELF-DRIVING CARS

Technology is also changing how people drive. Automobile makers are experimenting with self-driving cars. This technology would allow people to get into a car, select a destination, and sit back and relax as the car drives. Self-driving cars can travel anywhere, from wide-open highways to crowded city streets.

Several systems work together in a self-driving car. Lasers and cameras are mounted on the car. They can detect pedestrians, cars, and other obstacles. The information they capture goes to the car's computer. The computer then tells the car how to steer. It also makes the car speed up, slow down, or brake.

Some experts estimate that 60 percent of cars on the road will be self-driving by 2030. The hope is that self-driving cars will improve driver safety. The US Department of Transportation found that 37,461 drivers were killed on US roads in 2016. Self-driving cars would eliminate human error that often causes these car crashes. Unlike human drivers, self-driving cars do not text, talk, or eat while driving. They do not get road rage. And these cars have sensors that can take in more information than human ears and eyes. Despite this, many people are wary of turning control of their cars over to computers.

FURTHER EVIDENCE

Chapter Two discusses the United States as a nation of drivers. Identify one of the chapter's main points. What evidence is included to support this point? Read the article at the website below. Does the information on the website support an existing piece of evidence in the chapter? Or does it offer a new piece of evidence?

MILLENNIAL AND GEN X DRIVING TRENDS
abdocorelibrary.com/designing-city-transport

CHAPTER
THREE

MOVING THE MASSES

I n many cities, people use mass transit to travel short distances every day. Mass transit is a way to move many people in one vehicle, such as a bus or train. Mass transit is most useful in areas with many residents and workers. Enough commuters in these areas rely on this mode of transport to make the investment in mass transit worthwhile.

Mass transit has many benefits. All riders share the cost, which keeps ticket prices relatively low. In many cities, especially in Europe, it can be expensive to own and maintain a car. Some countries have also not invested enough in highway networks

More than 4 million people ride the New York City subway system each day.

25

to make driving an efficient mode of transportation. For these reasons, mass transit can be more efficient than driving. Riders may arrive at their destinations sooner than drivers could. Mass transit vehicles use less energy and emit less air pollution per person than cars.

Using mass transit is not always convenient, though. Buses, trains, and ferries run on a schedule. People can travel only during scheduled times. And mass transit vehicles go only to specific stops. The nearest stop

An elevated train system in Chicago, Illinois, runs above the crowded city streets.

may be far from the place a rider needs to go. Trains and buses can also be loud and crowded, and they may run late. Buses also use the same roads as other street traffic. Commuting by bus may be slower than commuting by car due to traffic delays.

HEAVY RAIL

In large cities, local trains are the heart of mass transit. They move many passengers in a fast, reliable manner. Each year, riders worldwide take approximately 3 billion trips on these trains. The trains quickly transport riders from one part of a city to another. They may be called metros, subways, or elevated trains. Because they can transport many people at once, these modes of transportation are called heavy rail.

Local trains are designed with speed in mind. They have their own right of way. This means they do not come into contact with other traffic. They do not have to wait for cars, pedestrians, or stoplights. Rails may run under city streets or above the city.

Rapid transit systems have many stops in a city. To decide where to place the stops, planners use geometry. They center an imaginary circle around each stop. This circle is called a walk radius. It is the distance a person would typically be willing to walk to a train stop. Planners then determine how many people in a walk radius might use the transit system. Knowing these factors allows them to determine where to locate stations.

COMMUTER AND LIGHT RAIL

Other forms of travel within cities include commuter rail and light rail transit (LRT). Commuter rail is a train service that runs at the street level. It transports people longer distances, from the city center to suburbs. LRT vehicles are powered by overhead electrical wires. They run on a system of railways that travel through cities. LRT railways run alongside roads.

PARATRANSIT

Many types of mass transit vehicles are equipped to accommodate people with limited mobility. Lifts and ramps allow people with wheelchairs, scooters, or walkers easy access to elevated buses and trains. If a person is physically unable to take a regularly scheduled bus or train, he or she can turn to paratransit. This is a public system that uses small, specially equipped buses and vans. A rider can call or text to request a ride. Drivers pick up passengers at their homes. They help the passengers get on and off the vehicles. This gives people with limited mobility greater independence.

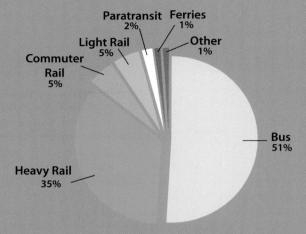

MASS TRANSIT IN THE UNITED STATES

Paratransit
2%

Ferries
1%

Light Rail
5%

Other
1%

Commuter
Rail
5%

Bus
51%

Heavy Rail
35%

The above graph shows the popularity of mass transit options within the United States in 2014 based on the number of trips taken. Why might some options be more popular than others?

They are separate from street traffic. LRT vehicles do not have to stop for other traffic. They have their own right of way. Because they run on electricity, LRT trains are quiet and emit hardly any pollution. These qualities have made LRT the fastest-growing type of rail travel in many countries.

BUSES

Unlike LRT and subways, buses can reach riders anywhere roads exist. They do not need any special infrastructure. Bus fares are generally low. Bus systems are the most-used form of mass transit. Buses carry approximately half of all mass transit riders.

In most cities, buses run on regular roads along with cars and trucks. Some cities are trying new ways to make commuting by bus faster and more reliable. They are using a system called bus rapid transit (BRT). BRT includes special lanes that only buses can use. Riders pay their fares at stations before boarding the bus. These changes make BRT faster than regular bus systems.

EXPLORE ONLINE

Chapter Three discusses modern types of mass transit. The article at the website below goes into more depth on this topic. In what ways are new forms of mass transit similar to the buses and trains people have been using for the past century? In what ways are they different?

TECHNOLOGY AND MASS TRANSIT
abdocorelibrary.com/designing-city-transport

PEOPLE POWER

Across the country, city planners are recognizing new needs. Residents are searching for alternatives to clogged highways. Many are interested in exercising while also running errands or going to work. And many residents want ways to travel that are good for the environment. To make these wishes a reality, city planners are trying to make walking and biking in cities safer and easier.

It is not an easy job to transform cities, but it can be done. One way planners are doing this is by creating what are called skinny streets. In Portland, Oregon, city planners

Wide sidewalks with buffers between pedestrians and busy streets make for easy walkability.

require residential streets to be only 20 to 26 feet (6 to 8 m) wide. In the past, some residential streets in Portland were as wide as 32 feet (10 m). Drivers naturally tend to travel more slowly on narrow streets, so walking is safer. And the extra space can be used to add sidewalks or bike lanes.

Adding features such as skinny streets shifts the focus from cars to people. This shift is part of a planning movement called New Urbanism. Its core goal is to build cities with a rich mix of homes, shops, offices, schools, parks, and restaurants all in a close area. These neighborhoods make it easy for residents to meet their daily needs without using a car. Today, more than 4,000 New Urbanism projects are in development within the United States.

WALKABILITY

A key concept in New Urbanism is walkability. Walkability is the ease with which a resident can travel by foot. Cities with high walkability make pedestrians

Bridges in large cities may have pedestrian walkways for people on foot to cross.

feel safe and comfortable. They provide easy access to places people visit often, such as banks and libraries. Walkable cities also give pedestrians easy access to other forms of transportation, such as buses and trains.

Cities with high walkability have many benefits. Walking is free. It is available to people of all ages and social classes. It does not require a license or equipment. Walking helps people stay fit and reduces stress. Walkable cities often have a strong sense of community. Residents are more likely to participate in local government and know their neighbors.

Walking also has a low impact on the environment. When the number of cars on city streets decreases, so do traffic levels. This reduces air and noise pollution. Driving less also decreases the amount of gas used to fuel cars. As a result, walkers save money and energy.

FEELING SAFE

To make a city walkable, planners must make pedestrians feel safe. Installing sidewalks is the most important way to do this. Wide sidewalks provide a protected, open area for pedestrians. Planners often include a buffer, or barrier, between the sidewalk and the road for extra safety. This area usually has trees, planters, or benches.

Pedestrians must also feel safe crossing the street. Well-designed crosswalks make this possible. A basic crosswalk has two painted lines on a road indicating where pedestrians may cross. Some cities paint crosswalks with patterns or use paint with reflective glass beads to make them more visible. In areas with heavy traffic, signs and flashing lights alert drivers to crosswalks and also improve safety.

Planting shade trees along sidewalks keeps pedestrians cool on hot days. Placing benches along sidewalks gives pedestrians a place to rest. Bright streetlights make walking outside at night safer. Lowering speed limits keeps traffic quieter and makes crossing streets easier.

TIMING THE LIGHTS

Traffic lights help pedestrians cross busy roads. They flash a "Walk" signal when crossing is safe. They flash a "Don't Walk" signal when cars are about to enter the crosswalk. A mathematical formula determines the timing of these signals. An average person walks at a rate of approximately 3.5 feet per second (1 m/s). Planners multiply this rate by the length of the crosswalk. The result determines how long the traffic light will flash the walk signal.

In some cities, cyclists bike next to cars in their own specially-designated lanes.

ON TWO WHEELS

Safety is also a key concern for bikers. A variety of bike routes exist in modern cities. Off-street paths are found in parks or other open public areas. They are free from car traffic. In crowded areas, designers may add a narrow bike lane on the street. It runs between street traffic and the curb.

Traveling entirely by bicycle is not always an option. The distance may be too far, or part of the route may be unsafe for cyclists. So people often combine bicycling with mass transit. They bike to a bus stop where they catch a city bus equipped with a bike rack. When they exit the bus, they can continue biking to their destination. Many subways and metros offer this service, too.

Many modern cities have bike sharing systems, which allow people to rent bicycles. People go to self-serve stations where they can pay to use a bike for a short period of time. If workers commute by

PERSPECTIVES

BICYCLES VERSUS CARS

As bicycling has become more popular, a heated debate has begun. Should bicycles be allowed on the same roads as cars? Critics say many bicyclists do not follow traffic laws, such as obeying stop signs or signaling a turn. Bicyclists often respond by saying the laws need to change. They say it doesn't make sense for small, slow bicycles to follow the same rules as heavy, fast-moving cars.

train, they can rent a bike to run errands at lunch. Or college students may take a bus to campus and then rent a bike to travel between classes.

Relying on bicycles as transportation is a fairly new idea in the United States. But people have been doing it for many years in Europe. Copenhagen, Denmark, is one of the world's best cycling cities. There, leaders have invested millions of dollars in bike infrastructure. This includes elevated bike lanes and bike highways. Today, more than 50 percent of trips within Copenhagen are taken by bike.

For many city planners, examples such as Copenhagen are inspiring. Planners hope to make as many transportation options as possible available to residents. When all of these transportation systems are working together smoothly, a city and its residents thrive.

STRAIGHT TO THE
SOURCE

Bicycle engineer Zach Krapfl designs electric bicycles. An electric bicycle has an electric motor that helps power the bike. In 2016, Krapfl gave a speech about the benefits of bikes as a form of transportation:

> *There are alternatives [to cars] out there that currently exist and if you go to places like Copenhagen or Amsterdam you find this unbelievable cycling infrastructure where the [bicycle] lanes are protected from the cars and they have priority. . . . In our culture, bicycles have mostly been used for . . . recreation, and if we foster . . . a generation that can see the bicycle as a mode of transportation, they are going to demand that we have bike infrastructure and demand that we continue this just like what we see in Copenhagen.*

Source: "Change in Your Transportation Future." *YouTube*. TEDx Talks, April 13, 2016. Web. Accessed September 22, 2017.

Changing Minds

Many Americans think of bicycling as a form of exercise but not as an efficient mode of transportation. How would you argue in favor of biking as an efficient mode of transportation?

FAST FACTS

- Efficient, safe, and useful transportation systems are the heart of a thriving city.

- Civil engineers and transportation planners design bike routes, pedestrian paths, roads, and mass transit systems in cities.

- Beginning in the 1950s, US transportation systems focused on cars and large networks of roads.

- To solve traffic problems, engineers are coming up with new solutions. These include smart stoplights, high-occupancy vehicle lanes, and bus rapid transit lanes.

- Mass transit systems, such as subways and buses, are efficient ways to move large numbers of people in a city.

- Mass transit can be cheaper, cleaner, and faster than driving.

- More cities are installing bike lanes to allow workers to commute by bicycle rather than by car.

- Today's city planners are focusing more on the experiences of pedestrians when planning streets.

- When people feel comfortable and safe on city streets, they are more likely to walk than to drive.

STOP AND
THINK

Say What?

Building transportation systems involves many specialized fields, each with its own terms. Find three transportation-related words you've never heard before. Use a dictionary to find out what they mean. Then write the meanings in your own words, and use each word in a sentence.

Surprise Me

Chapter Three discusses different types of mass transit. After reading this chapter, what two or three facts about mass transit surprised you most? Write a few sentences about each fact. Why did you find each fact surprising?

Take a Stand

Chapter Four discusses the trend toward making cities friendlier for walkers and bicyclists. Make a list with at least three pros and three cons of making these changes. Then write a few sentences with your opinion on the issue.

Dig Deeper

After reading this book, what kinds of transportation systems can you identify in your own city? With an adult's help, research your city's transportation systems. What kinds of systems exist in your city and why were they created? Write a paragraph to explain what you've learned.

GLOSSARY

commute
to travel back and forth between work and home

compact
to press together

drainage
the process of removing water from streets by using a network of drains

elevation
a drawing of a structure from a specific viewpoint

Global Positioning System (GPS)
a navigation system that involves satellites in space sending radio waves to a phone or other device on Earth

infrastructure
the structures and systems a city needs to run

pedestrian
a person who travels on foot

perspective
the point from which something is viewed

right of way
a road that is reserved for a specific purpose, such as a bus lane

suburb
a community that is just outside a city

urbanologist
someone who studies cities and city planning

ONLINE RESOURCES

To learn more about designing city transport, visit our free resource websites below.

Visit **abdocorelibrary.com** for free Common Core resources for teachers and students, including vetted activities, multimedia, and booklinks, for deeper subject comprehension.

Visit **abdobooklinks.com** for free additional online weblinks for further learning. These links are routinely monitored and updated to provide the most current information available.

LEARN MORE

Green, Oliver. *Firefly Encyclopedia of Transportation*. Ontario, Canada: Firefly Books, 2017.

Hancock, James Gulliver. *How Cities Work*. Oakland, CA: Lonely Planet Kids, 2016.

INDEX

About the Author

Kate Conley has been writing nonfiction books for children for more than ten years. When she's not writing, Conley spends her time reading, sewing, and solving crossword puzzles. She lives in Minnesota with her husband and two children.